Y0-BUK-437

Cooking For One:
One Pot, *Slow Cooker Recipes -* *Easy Recipes for One*

By
Kristina Newman

Copyright © 2015 KMT Publishers, Inc.

This document is geared towards providing exact and reliable information in regards to the topic and issue covered. The publication is sold with the idea that the publisher is not required to render accounting, officially permitted, or otherwise, qualified services. If advice is necessary, legal or professional, a practiced individual in the profession should be ordered.

From a Declaration of Principles which was accepted and approved equally by a Committee of the American Bar Association and a Committee of Publishers and Associations.

In no way is it legal to reproduce, duplicate, or transmit any part of this document in either electronic means or in printed format. Recording of this publication is strictly prohibited and any storage of this document is not allowed unless with written permission from the publisher. All rights reserved.

The information provided herein is stated to be truthful and consistent, in that any liability, in terms of inattention or otherwise, by any usage or abuse of any policies, processes, or directions contained within is the solitary and utter responsibility of the recipient reader. Under no circumstances will any legal responsibility or blame be held against the publisher for any reparation, damages, or monetary loss due to the information herein, either directly or indirectly.

Respective authors own all copyrights not held by the publisher. The information herein is offered for informational purposes solely, and is universal as so. The presentation of the information is without contract or any type of guarantee assurance.

The trademarks that are used are without any consent, and the publication of the trademark is without permission or backing by the trademark owner. All trademarks and brands within this book are for clarifying purposes only and are the owned by the owners themselves, not affiliated with this document.

Table of Contents

Introduction

Congratulations and Thank You!

I want to start by thanking you for downloading the book, *"Cooking For One: One Pot, Slow Cooker Recipes - Easy Recipes for One."* I am honored to be helping you on this journey to create quick & easy Recipes For One!

One of the best feelings in the world is the ability to prepare a delicious, healthy meal for yourself. The comfort foods that we cling to can be nostalgic for us as we think about what was served in our families growing up, and we therefore try to replicate them as best as possible to recreate that warm feeling with every bite. Yet it can be difficult in making sure that all the components are there, especially if you are not cooking for a whole family, but for only one person. The ingredients and the preparation can seem challenging if you have to constantly divide the proportions to get it just right for a serving size of one. And if you find yourself strapped for time, the process can get even more stressful.

Fortunately, there is an answer, and it is located right in this book. As you flip through the pages and study the recipes, you'll notice that the math and the directions are all done for you so that you can get on with preparing tasty meals for yourself. Your time is taken into consideration, as well, seeing as these meals are not prepared in just any old way. The benefit of the following recipes is that they are all prepared using a slow cooker, one of the most convenient culinary inventions to ever make its way into a kitchen. Slow cookers allow you to place the majority or all of your ingredients into one container, set the temperature, and leave them to cook for the recommended amount of time. This "set it and forget it" procedure has made cooking a much less stressful process, and in the end, you'll have a delectable meal that you can be proud to serve! Unlock all the flavors of slow cooked meals with these recipes you're sure to enjoy.

This book contains proven recipes and tips on how you can make quick, easy Recipes for One. It will provide you with everything you need to know from tools, ingredients, and recipes to storage.

Thanks again for downloading this book, I Hope You Enjoy It

50 Cooking For One Slow Cooker Recipes

Here you will find fun and easy Cooking For One Recipes, Enjoy!!

Cooking For One Slow Cooker Mexican Chicken

INGREDIENTS:
1/2 medium white or yellow onion, sliced
2 boneless, skinless chicken thighs
1/2 tsp. Mexican seasoning blend
Pinch of salt
1 Tbsps. olive oil
1/2 large ear corn on the cob, cut into 4 pieces (optional)
1/4 cup chicken broth
1 Tbsp. prepared mole sauce
1 Tbsps. creamy peanut butter
1 Tbsps. dark brown sugar
1/2 Tbsp. chocolate syrup
1/8 tsp. red pepper flakes
1 tsps. sesame seeds, toasted

INSTRUCTIONS:
Use a cooking spray to coat slow cooker.
Spread the white or yellow onion slices in the bottom of the slow cooker.
Rub the chicken with the salt and Mexican seasoning.
Pour the oil in a skillet, add the chicken and cook for about 3 minutes until a nice brown in color.
Turn the meat and allow the other side to brown.
Transfer the meat to the slow cooker with the smooth side facing upwards.
Toss in the corn pieces around the meat, if using.
Combine the mole sauce, broth, peanut butter, chocolate syrup, sugar and pepper flakes in a bowl using a fork.
Place the bowl in the microwave and warm until the peanut butter starts melting a little.
Sprinkle the mole sauce over the meat inside the slow cooker.
Cover with lid and cook for 3 hours on high or 6 hours on low.
Transfer the meat and the corn using a large spoon to a dish.
Sprinkle a dash of sesame seeds on top.

Cooking for One Pepper Steak Slow Cooker

INGREDIENTS:
1/2 onion thinly sliced
1/2 green pepper thinly sliced
1/4 red pepper thinly sliced
1/2 pounds beef roast, sliced against the grain
1/2 tb Soy Sauce
1/2 tb Sesame oil
Salt and pepper to taste
1/2 tsp Brown Sugar
1 garlic cloves thinly sliced

INSTRUCTIONS:
Place the vegetables in the slow cooker.
Toss in the meat and seasonings and combine well.
Cover with lid and cook for 2 hours until the ingredients are cooked.

Cooking for One Artichoke Lemon Chicken Soup

INGREDIENTS:
.25 lbs. boneless skinless chicken breast
3 oz. canned artichoke hearts, packed in water, drained (frozen works as well)
1/8 onion, diced
1/4 carrots, diced
1/4 celery ribs, diced
1/2 garlic cloves, minced
1/8 bay leaf
1/8 tsp. salt
1/8 tsp. pepper
1/4 cup long grain rice (not quick cooking)
1 cups low-sodium chicken broth
1/8 cup freshly squeezed lemon juice
1/8 cup parsley, chopped

INSTRUCTIONS:
Place all the ingredients other than the parsley and the lemon juice in the slow cooker.
Cook for 8 hours on low.
Transfer the chicken onto a flat surface and shred using a fork.
Return the shredded meat into the slow cooker.
Adjust seasonings prior to serving.
Finally, add the parsley and lemon juice and combine well.

Cooking for One Slow Cooker Chicken Musakhan

INGREDIENTS:
.5 lbs boneless skinless chicken thighs
1/4 onions, halved lengthwise and thinly sliced
.25 Tbs olive oil
0.5 oz (weight) ground sumac*
1/4 tsp cinnamon
1/8 tsp ground allspice
1/8 tsp ground cloves
Big pinch saffron (optional, but nice)
Handful of pine nuts
Fresh mint for garnish (optional)
Salt and pepper

INSTRUCTIONS:
Place the onions, sumac, cinnamon, allspice, cloves and saffron in a microwave proof bowl.
Add the olive oil and microwave for 3 minutes and then again for another 2 minutes.
Dump the chicken thighs into the Slow Cooker.
Sprinkle salt and pepper.
Toss in the onion mixture and cook for 2 hours on low.
Just before serving, sauté the pine nuts in olive oil and leave until brown.
Chop the mint for garnishing.
Adjust seasoning, if required and sprinkle with pine nuts and mint.

Cooking for One Slow Cooker Spicy Pork Chops

INGREDIENTS:
1 boneless Pork chops (3/4" thick)
1/2 chicken bouillon cube
1/8 cup hot water
1 Tbsp Grey Poupon Mustard
1 small onions
freshly ground pepper

INSTRUCTIONS:
Sear both sides of the pork chops.
Dissolve the soup cube with a bit of hot water and mix with the mustard.
Skin the onions and cut into 2" thick wheels.
Insert the onions into the bottom of the slow cooker in one layer.
Place the chops on top of the onions.
Add a bit of ground pepper on top.
Pour the liquid over the ingredients.
Cook for about 5 hours until the ingredients are done.

Cooking for One Slow Cooker Saucy Steak Dinner

INGREDIENTS:
1/2 lb. round steak, cut into 1inch thick and
1/8inch wide strips
1/8 c. chopped onions
1/8 c. chopped celery
1/8 c. water
1/4 tsp. Worcestershire sauce
1/4 can mushrooms, drained (save liquid)
1/8 c. French dressing
¼ pkg. sour cream sauce mix

INSTRUCTIONS:
Place the steak pieces in the pot.
Top up with onions, mushrooms and celery.
Prepare the dressing by mixing the sour cream mix,
Worcestershire sauce, mushroom liquid and water in a bowl.
Pour the contents of the bowl into the pot.
Allow to simmer for 1 hour on medium.
Maintain the warmth over a low setting and serve with noodles.

Cooking for One Slow Cooker Smothered Silky Steak

INGREDIENTS:
1/2 lb round or Swiss steak, 3/4 thick
salt pepper
1/2 small onion, thinly sliced
2 oz can tomato sauce (I use canned tomatoes)

INSTRUCTIONS:
Slice the steak in half and rub salt and pepper.
Insert the slices of onion in the Slow Cooker.
Top up with the meat and pour the tomato sauce over the ingredients.
Cover with lid and cook for about 1 hour.

Cooking for One Slow Cooker Puerco Pibil

INGREDIENTS:
¼ medium onion
3 oz. can of diced fire-roasted tomato
1/2 Tbsp annato powder (sub paprika if you can't find annato)
1/4 tsp ground cumin
1/4 tsp ground black pepper
1/4 tsp salt
Pinch of nutmeg
2 lb pork shoulder roast
1/4 orange, juiced
1/8 cup apple cider vinegar
1/2 tsp salt

INSTRUCTIONS:
Combine the annatto, black pepper, cumin, ¼ tsp salt and a dash of nutmeg in a bowl.
Add a bit of water and form a thick paste.
Cut the onion into slices and sauté in a bit of coconut oil.
Cook until the onion is tender and mix with the tomatoes.
Allow to cook for a few minutes until the ingredients are soft.
Trim the pork of any unnecessary fat.
Cut the pork into 1.5" wide slices.
Rub the pork with salt.
Pour the orange juice and cider vinegar into the Slow Cooker.
Add the annatto and paste and stir until well dissolved.
Add the pork into the mixture.
Lay the tomato/onion mix on top and cook for 2-4 hours.
Take out the excess fat from the surface when it remains warm or can be refrigerated where the solid fat can be removed.
Can be served for breakfast with a couple of eggs.

Cooking for One Honey Garlic Chicken Wings in the Slow Cooker

INGREDIENTS:
2 pc. Chicken wings
1/4 cup of raw honey (preferably liquid or melted)
1/8 tbsp of minced garlic
1/2 tbsp of olive oil
1/8 tsp sea salt
1/8 tsp pepper

INSTRUCTIONS:
Insert the chicken wings into the Slow Cooker.
Combine the honey, olive oil, garlic, salt and pepper in a bowl until liquid.
Add the mixture on top of the chicken wings.
Cook for 1 hour on low.

Cooking for One Slow Cooker Vegetable Beef Soup

INGREDIENTS:

1/2 lb stew meat, cut into 1/2 inch cubes
1/2 can (14 oz) tomatoes
1/2 carrot, sliced
1/2 small onion, diced
1/2 stalk celery, sliced
1/4 cup frozen mixed veggies
Salt & Pepper
1/2 beef bouillon cube
water

INSTRUCTIONS:

Place all the ingredients in the Slow Cooker.
Pour the water just sufficient to cover the ingredients.
Combine well.
Cover with lid and cook for 2 hours until the ingredients are done.

Cooing for One Slow Cooker Cashew Chicken

INGREDIENTS:
4 - oz. can condensed golden mushroom soup
1 Tbsps. soy sauce
1/4 tsp. ground ginger
1/2 pounds chicken tenders
4 - oz. package frozen broccoli stir-fry vegetable blend
1 - oz. can (drained weight) sliced mushrooms, drained
1/2 cup cashews
Hot cooked brown rice (optional)

INSTRUCTIONS:
Mix the soy sauce, mushroom soup and ginger.
Add the chicken, mushrooms and the stir-fry vegetables.
Cover with lid and cook for 1 hour on low.
Toss in the cashews with the chicken.
Serve warm with cooked rice.

Cooking for One Slow Cooker Balsamic Sausage & Chicken

INGREDIENTS:
1 boneless, skinless chicken breasts (don't hate me for that)
1 fresh Italian sausage links (sweet or spicy or a combo is fine)
1/4 white onion, thinly sliced (not diced!)
1 cloves of garlic, chopped
Extra virgin olive oil
1/4 tsp Italian seasoning
1/4 tsp garlic powder
1/4 tsp kosher salt
1/2 oz cans organic diced tomatoes
5 oz can tomato sauce
1/4 cup water or chicken stock
1/8 cup balsamic vinegar
+ 1/4 tsp Italian seasoning
+ 1/8 tsp kosher salt
+ 1/8 tsp garlic powder

INSTRUCTIONS:
Place the chicken breasts in the bottom of the slow cooker.
Rub a bit of olive oil on top.
Add the Italian, garlic powder and salt directly onto the meat without mixing.
Spread the sausages over the seasoned meat.
Lay the sliced onion and chopped garlic on top.
Stir in the diced tomatoes, tomato sauce, balsamic vinegar and water/stock into the slow cooker.
Add the next round of seasonings without mixing and just sprinkle on top.
Cover with lid and cook for 5 hours on high.

Cooking for One Apple Brown Betty Slow Cooker

INGREDIENTS:
2 slices of bread, cubed
1/4 c Butter, melted
1/8 tsp Cinnamon
dash Nutmeg
dash Salt
1 1/2 tbls Brown sugar, firmly packed
1 c Cooking apples, peel and chop

INSTRUCTIONS:
Place the bread cubes in a bowl.
Add the butter, nutmeg, cinnamon, brown sugar and salt into the bowl.
Lay the bread mixture and apples in alternate layers in the slow cooker.
Cover with lid and cook for 3 hours until the fruits are tender.
Can be served with hard sauce, cream or ice cream, as desired.

Cooking for One Slow Cooker Apple Pork Tenderloin

INGREDIENTS:
1 Organic Gala Apples
½lbPork Tenderloin
Nutmeg
1/2 Tbsp Raw Honey (optional)

INSTRUCTIONS:
Core and cut the apples into slices.
Place a layer of apple slices in the slow cooker and add a dash of nutmeg on top.
Make slits in the meat and cut the tenderloin in half.
Slice one apple and place in each cut of the meat.
Insert the meat with apple slices into the slow cooker.
Add the balance apple slices on top of the stuffed pork.
Sprinkle more nutmeg on top.
Leave the slow cooker on low and leave for a few hours until the dinner is cooked and ready to be served.

Cooking for One Slow Cooker Fajita Chicken

INGREDIENTS:
1 pounds skinless, boneless chicken (breast, thighs or a combination)
1/4 small onion, sliced thin
1 cloves garlic, minced
1/2 cups bell peppers, sliced
1/4 tsp kosher salt
1/4 tsp ground coriander
1/4 tsp dried oregano
1/8 tsp cumin
1/8 tsp chipotle chili powder
5 oz can of diced tomatoes

INSTRUCTIONS:
Spread the chicken in the bottom of the slow cooker.
Chop the onion and bell peppers and mince the garlic.
Place the above ingredients over the meat.
Add the dry ingredients on top.
Finally add the diced tomatoes without mixing.
Cover with lid and cook for about ½ hour on high and 1 hour on low.
Shred the meat using a fork.

Cooking for One Cinnamon Savory Slow Cooker Chicken

INGREDIENTS:

1/2 lb. chicken breasts (you can use legs or thighs if you prefer.)
1/4 Bell Peppers sliced. (I used one green and one orange.)
1/8 Onion diced
1/4 tsp. Paprika
1 Cloves garlic minced
1/2 tsp cinnamon
1/4 c. Chicken broth
1/8 tsp. Nutmeg Step

INSTRUCTIONS:

Place all ingredients in a zip-lock freezer bag.
Ensure to remove the air and seal the bag.
Take out the meal from the freezer and thaw overnight in the refrigerator.
Dump the contents of the bag into the slow cooker and cook for a while on low.

Cooking for One Apple Juice Ham Slow Cooker

INGREDIENTS:
1/2 lb. canned ham
1/2 c. apple juice
1/3 c. brown sugar
1/2 tsp. prepared mustard

INSTRUCTIONS:
Cut the ham into two slices and place in a slow cooker.
Add the brown sugar, mustard and the apple juice and combine well.
Cover with lid and cook until done.

Cooking for One Slow Cooker Beef with Pepper Sauce

INGREDIENTS:
Tongue
1/2 beef tongue
1/4 onion, sliced
1/2 garlic cloves, crushed
1/2 bay leaves
Sea salt and pepper
Water to cover tongue in slow cooker
Sauce
1/4 roasted red pepper, peeled and diced
1/4 roasted serrano chili pepper, diced
1/4 onion, diced
3/4 garlic cloves, minced
5 oz. tomatoes, sliced
2 oz. tomato paste
1/4 tsp thyme
1/4 tsp oregano
Salt and pepper to taste

INSTRUCTIONS:
Wash and pat dry the beef tongue.
Lay onion, bay leaves and garlic in the bottom of the slow cooker.
Place the beef tongue on top and rub with salt and pepper.
Add sufficient water to cover the ingredients.
Cover with lid and cook for 8 hours on low.
Transfer from the cooker and peel off the skin from the tongue.
Use a fork and shred the beef.
Prepare the sauce – Sauté the onions, red pepper, garlic and chile until soft.
Toss in the balance ingredients and mix well.
Lower the heat and allow to simmer for 30 minutes.
If you want to make a smooth sauce, insert into a blender and process until smooth.
Serve the beef with sauce.

Cooking for One Mirepoix Slow Cooker Chicken

INGREDIENTS:
1/4 whole chicken
Sea salt
Crushed white pepper
1/4 small onion, chopped
1/2 carrots, peeled and diced
1/2 stalks of celery, diced
1 cloves of garlic, peeled and smashed
2 sprigs of fresh thyme, 3 diced
Juice of 1/2 lemon

INSTRUCTIONS:
Rinse the chicken in cold water and pat dry using kitchen towels.
Season the inside and outside of the meat with sea salt and a bit of crushed white pepper.
Lay half the quantity of the diced veggies in the slow cooker and spread the chicken on top.
Insert a clove of garlic and 2 sprigs of thyme into the chicken.
Sprinkle the chopped thyme and the balance veggies on top of the chicken.
Add a bit of lemon juice over the meat and place the halves of the lemon inside the chicken.
Place the chicken in the slow cooker and cook for 1 hour on low.
Shred the meat and remove the bones.
Transfer the meat into the slow cooker and serve with shredded veggies.
Serve with grilled BBQ Asparagus and enjoy!

Cooking for One Baked Beans Slow Cooker

INGREDIENTS:

8 oz pork and beans with sauce

1/3 cup brown sugar

1/2 tsp prepared mustard

1/2 tsp dry minced onion

1 slices bacon fried crisp and crumbled

1/8 cup catsup

INSTRUCTIONS:

Place the beans in a slow cooker.

Add the balance ingredients and combine well.

Cover with lid and cook for 2 hours.

Cooking for One Slow Cooker Mushroom Chicken Cacciatore

INGREDIENTS:
1 boneless, skinless chicken thighs
1 boneless chicken drumsticks, skin removed
4 oz. can tomato sauce
1/8 cup tomato paste
1/2 jars sliced mushrooms, drained
1/4 onions, chopped
1 cloves garlic, minced
1/2 green bell peppers, chopped
1/4 tsp. dried Italian seasoning
1/2 Tbsp. flour
1/8 red wine or chicken broth
1/4 Tbsp. red wine vinegar
1/8 tsp. dried oregano

INSTRUCTIONS:
Slice the chicken drumsticks and thighs into 1" pieces.
Mix all the ingredients other than the flour, wine, vinegar and oregano in a slow cooker.
Combine well.
Cover with lid and cook for 1 hour on low until the meat is cooked.
Place the wine, vinegar, flour and dried oregano.
Pour the mixture over the chicken and combine well.
Cover with lid and cook for 10 minutes on high until the mixture is thickened.
Serve warm with cooked egg noodles.

Cooking for One Slow Cooker Chicken and Shrimp

INGREDIENTS:

1/4 pound boneless, skinless chicken thighs
1/8 tsp. salt
1/8 tsp. pepper
1/8 tsp. crushed red pepper flakes
1/4 onions, chopped
1 cloves garlic, minced
3 oz. can seasoned diced tomatoes
1 Tbsps. tomato paste
1/4 cup chicken broth
1/4 tsp. dried thyme leaves
1/8 tsp. dried basil leaves
1 Tbsps. lemon juice
2 oz. package frozen cooked shrimp, thawed
4 oz. can artichoke hearts, drained and chopped
1/4 Tbsp. cornstarch
1/8 cup crumbled feta cheese

INSTRUCTIONS:

Slice the chicken into chunks and rub with seasonings.
Lay the onion and garlic in the bottom of a slow cooker and top up with the meat.
Mix the tomatoes with the liquid, tomato paste, thyme, basil, broth and lemon juice in a bowl.
Pour the mixture over the chicken.
Cover with lid and cook for 1 hour on low until the meat is tender.
Toss in the shrimp, artichoke hearts coated with cornstarch.
Cover and cook for another 10 minutes until well heated and thickened.
Serve with pasta or couscous and sprinkle feta cheese on top.

Cooking for One Slow Cooker Roast Dinner

INGREDIENTS:
1/2Tbsp. flour
1/4 tsp. salt
1/8 tsp. pepper
1/4 tsp. dried marjoram leaves
1/8tsp. dried thyme leaves
1/2 lb. boneless beef top round, cut into 6 pieces
1/4 Tbsp. olive oil
1 potatoes, peeled, cut into chunks
(4 oz. pkg. baby carrots
1/4 onion, chopped
(4 oz.) Can ready to serve beef broth
1/8 cup water
1/4 Tbsp. Worcestershire sauce
1/2 Tbsp. cornstarch
1/8 cup water

INSTRUCTIONS:
Mix the flour, pepper, salt, marjoram and thyme in a bowl.
Toss in the beef and mix well.
Pour olive into a skillet and heat well.
Sauté the beef for about 3 minutes per side and allow both sides
to brown.
Leave aside.
Mix the potatoes, onion and carrots in a slow cooker.
Place the beef on vegetables and pour the broth over the
ingredients.
Add the Worcestershire sauce and water and combine well.
Cover with lid and cook until the ingredients are done.

Cooking for One Chili Verde Slow Cooker

INGREDIENTS:
1/2 tsps. olive oil
1/2 Tbsps. onion, chopped
1/4 cloves garlic, minced
1/4 lb boneless pork shoulder, cubed
1/8 cup green salsa
1/2 Tbsp. diced jalapeno peppers
1/4 cup diced canned tomatillos

INSTRUCTIONS:
Pour the oil into a skillet and heat well.
Toss in the onion and garlic and cook until fragrant.
Add the pork and cook for 4-6 minutes on each side until brown.
Remove the pork, onion and the garlic and place in a slow cooker.
Stir in the jalapeno peppers, tomatoes, and the salsa.
Cover with lid and cook for 2 hours on high.
Lower the heat to low and cook for another 3 hours.

Cooking for One Ham and Cabbage Dinner Slow Cooker

INGREDIENTS:
2 baby carrots
2 boiling onions
1/2 celery stalk
1/2 small turnip
[half a parsnip and or leek or potato]
sprig of parsley
peppercorns
1/8 cabbage
1/4 lb of a 1" ham steak
water

INSTRUCTIONS:
Chop the herbs and vegetables and place them in the bottom of the slow cooker.
Add the cabbage and ham over the ingredients.
Pour water just sufficiently to cover the ham.
Cook for about 2 hours until all the ingredients are done.

Cooking for One Slow Cooker Round Steak

INGREDIENTS:

1/4 round steak

1/2 cans cream of mushroom soup

1/4 envelope Lipton dry onion soup mix

INSTRUCTIONS:

Slice the steak into servable pieces.

Place the meat in the slow cooker.

Add the mushroom soup and onion soup mix and cook for 1 hour on low.

Toss in the carrots and potatoes and combine well.

Cooking for One Slow cooker Angel Chicken

INGREDIENTS:
1 skinless, boneless chicken breast halves (about 1-1/2 pounds)
1/4 Tbsp. vegetable oil (optional)
2 - oz. package fresh button mushrooms, quartered
2 - oz. package fresh shiitake mushrooms, stems removed, caps sliced
1/8 cup butter
0.3 - oz. package Italian dry salad dressing mix
4 - oz. can condensed golden mushroom soup
1/8 cup dry white wine
2 - oz. tub cream cheese spread with chives and onion
Hot cooked rice or angel hair pasta.
Snipped fresh chives or sliced green onions (optional)

INSTRUCTIONS:
Pour the oil in a skillet and brown on both sides.
Toss in the mushrooms into the slow cooker and top up with the meat.
Place the butter in a saucepan and melt well.
Add the Italian dressing mix and stir well.
Stir in the white wine, cream cheese and the mushroom soup and leave until the cheese starts melting.
Pour over the meat.
Cover with lid and cook for 1 hour on low.
Serve the meat with rice and if required garnish with chives.

Cooking for One Meat Loaf Slow Cooker

INGREDIENTS:
1/2 lb lean ground beef
1 egg
1/3 cup quick cooking oats
1TB dry onion soup mix
1/8 cup catsup

INSTRUCTIONS:
Mix the ground beef, oats, egg, soup mix and 3 tbsp of catsup in a bowl.
Form a loaf, using your hands.
Spread the balance catsup on top.
Place the ingredients in the slow cooker.
Cover with lid and cook for 1 hour.

Cook for One Slow cooker Super Simple Peachy Barbecue Chicken

INGREDIENTS:
2 pc chicken drumsticks, skinned (if desired)
1/2 cup barbecue sauce
1/3 cup apricot or peach preserves
1/2 tsps. yellow mustard
Fresh peaches, cut into wedges (optional)

INSTRUCTIONS:
Insert the meat into a slow cooker.
To make the sauce, mix the barbecue sauce, mustard and preserves.
Pour the sauce over the meat.
Cover with lid and cook for 1 hour on low.
Transfer the meat to platter and keep the meat warm.
Pour the sauce into a saucepan and allow the mixture to boil.
Lower the heat, simmer and leave for about 10 minutes until the sauce comes into the required consistency.
Serve the meat with the sauce.
Garnish with fresh peaches, if required.

Cooking for One Slow Cooker Cranberry Chicken

INGREDIENTS:
2 pc chicken thighs and/or drumsticks, skinned
4 - oz. can whole cranberry sauce
1/2 Tbsps. dry onion soup mix
1/2 Tbsps. quick-cooking tapioca
1/2 cups hot cooked rice

INSTRUCTIONS:
Place the meat in a bowl.
Add the cranberry sauce, dry soup mix and tapioca.
Pour the sauce over the meat.
Cover with lid and cook for 1 hour.
Can be served with sauce over hot cooked rice.

Cooking for One Mushroom Steak Slow Cooker

INGREDIENTS:
1/2 small steak (any round steak is good)
1/2 can cream of mushroom soup, add 1/2 soup can of water.
Salt, optional
pepper

INSTRUCTIONS:
Place the steak in the slow cooker and rub with salt and pepper.
Pour the soup on top of the steak and cook for about 1 hour.
Cam be served with rice or noodles.

Cooking for One Slow Cooker Apple Pie Steel-Cut Oatmeal

INGREDIENTS:

1/4 cup Steel-Cut Oats (certified gluten-free if necessary)
1 cups unsweetened Almond Milk (certified gluten-free if necessary)
1/2 medium Apples, chopped
1/4 tsp. Coconut Oil
1/4 tsp. Cinnamon
1/8 tsp. Nutmeg
1/2 Tbsp. Maple Syrup
Splash of Lemon Juice
Optional Toppings
Peanut Butter
Freshly chopped apples

INSTRUCTIONS:

Toss in all the ingredients into your slow cooker.
Stir well and cook for 8 hours on low or for 4 hours on high.
If desired, top up with chopped apples or peanut butter.
Leftovers, can be refrigerated and kept for 1 week.
At the time of re-heating, add a bit of almond milk and leave in the microwave to heat for a few seconds.

Cooking for One Slow Cooker Bacon, Egg & Hash brown Casserole

INGREDIENTS:
3 oz. bag frozen, shredded hash browns (I used Trader Joe's)
1 slices thick-cut bacon, cooked and coarsely chopped
1 oz. shredded cheddar cheese
1 green onions, sliced thin
1 eggs
1/8 cup milk
1/8 tsp. salt
1/8 tsp. pepper
Cooking oil (to lightly coat slow cooker)

INSTRUCTIONS:
Spray the slow cooker with a bit of oil.
Place half the quantity of the hash browns in the bottom of the slow cooker.
Add half the bacon, half the quantity of the cheese and 1/3rd of the green onions on top.
Keep aside a bit of bacon and little green onions for garnishing purposes.
Repeat with another layer of hash browns, bacon and cheese and onion.
Whisk the eggs, salt, pepper and milk in a bowl and pour over the top.
Cook till the eggs are firm for about 1 hour.
Sprinkle the balance bacon and onions on top and serve warm.
If preferred, can be served with hot sauce.

Cooking for One Slow Cooker Turkey Chili

INGREDIENTS:
.25 pounds 99% Lean Ground Turkey
1/4 tsp. Oil
1/4 medium Onion, minced
1/4 medium red Bell Pepper, diced fine
1/4 Garlic clove, minced
1/4 cups frozen Corn kernels
2 oz can Mild Diced Tomatoes
8 oz small can plain Tomato Sauce
1/8 cup low sodium Chicken Broth
1/4 tsp. Cumin
1/8 tsp. Chili Powder
1/8 tsp. Paprika
1/8 tsp. kosher Salt
Optional Garnishes
Diced Avocado
2% Greek Yogurt
Shredded Cheese
Baked Tortilla Chips
INSTRUCTIONS:
Pour oil into a skillet and heat well.
Add the ground turkey, rub with salt and brown the meat until cooked.
Place the cooked meat in the slow cooker.
Pour the oil into a skillet and temper the onion, bell pepper and garlic for about 5 minutes.
Spread the onion mixture over the slow cooker.
Add the corn, tomatoes, tomato sauce, chili powder, cumin, paprika and salt and combine well.
Pour the broth over the rest of the ingredients in the slow cooker and finally add the bay leaf.

Cooking for One Slow Cooker Jerk Chicken

INGREDIENTS:
1/4 cup of chopped Green Onions (approx. 2-3 stalks)
1/4 tsp. dried Thyme
1/4 Garlic Clove
1/8 tsp. Cayenne Pepper (or more if you like it really spicy)
1/4 tsp. ground Allspice
1/4 tsp. ground dried Mustard
1/8 tsp. Cinnamon
1/4 tsp. Salt
1/4 Tbsp. fresh Lemon Juice
1/4 Tbsp. Honey
1/2 pounds of Chicken Legs (approx. 10 drumsticks), with skin on or off as preference
1/4 tsp. Coconut or Olive oil for greasing slow cooker

INSTRUCTIONS:
Add the ingredients other than the meat and oil into a food processor.
Process until well combined.
Spray a slow cooker with a bit of oil and place the meat inside.
Spread the jerk mixture on top and cook for 4 hours on low.
Turn the chicken onto the other side to baste with the juice after about 1 hour of cooking time.
Prior to serving, set the oven to broil.
Transfer the meat onto a baking sheet and pour the balance juices on top.
Broil the meat until it is crisp and firm for 5 minutes.

Cooking For One Slow Cooker Lamb One Pot

INGREDIENTS:
1/12 carrots, peeled and cut into chunks
6small new potatoes
About 350g boneless lamb shoulder joint
Salt and pepper
200ml lamb stock (I used a stock cube)
1 Tbsps. Bisto® gravy granules
Mint sauce or jelly to serve
Yorkshire pudding to serve
INSTRUCTIONS:
Insert the potatoes and carrots into a slow cooker.
Discard any string left from the lamb and place the meat on top.
Rub with salt and pepper.
Pour the lamb stock over the ingredients.
Cover with lid and cook until tender.
Use a fork and shred the meat.
Make about 70ml water almost boiling with the Bisto and remove a few spoonful to taste.
Serve the lamb and vegetables with mint sauce, Yorkshire pudding and gravy.

Cooking For One Chicken Cacciatore In The Slow Cooker

INGREDIENTS:
1 skinless, boneless chicken breast fillets
100 jar tomato pasta sauce
1/4 green peppers, seeded and cubed
50g fresh mushrooms, sliced
1/4 onion, finely diced
1/4 cloves garlic, minced

INSTRUCTIONS:
Place the chicken breast fillets in the slow cooker.
Add the rest of the ingredients.
Cover with lid and cook for about 2 hours on low.

Cooking For One Slow Cooker Chicken And Mushroom Curry

INGREDIENTS:
2 chicken thigh pieces
1/2 chopped onion
1/2 tin condensed low fat mushroom soup
75g sliced mushrooms
1 tsps. curry powder (or to taste)
1 tsps. dried mixed herbs

INSTRUCTIONS:
Place the chicken in a skillet and brown on both sides.
Place the browned meat in a slow cooker.
Sauté the onions until soft and mix with the chicken.
Add the balance ingredients into the slow cooker and combine well.
Cook for a little over 3 hours.

Cooking for One Amazing Pork Fillet in the Slow Cooker

INGREDIENTS:
100g pork fillet
10g sachet onion soup mix
50ml water
40ml red wine
1/2 Tbsps. minced garlic
1/2 Tbsps. soy sauce

INSTRUCTIONS:
Insert the pork into a slow cooker.
Add the contents of the soup sachet.
Pour the soy sauce, wine and water over the ingredients and toss the meat to season well.
Gently rub the garlic on the pork and sprinkle a dash of pepper on top.
Cover with lid and cook for 1 hour on low.
Serve with the juices.

Cooking For One Slow Cooker Salmon

INGREDIENTS:
1 small onion, chopped
4 mushrooms, chopped
1/2 red pepper, chopped
1 tsp. margarine or butter
1 cup vegetable stock
1 tsp. chilli powder
1.5 oz rice
1 Tbsp. light soy sauce
1 Tbsp. lime juice
1 garlic cloves, crushed
1 salmon fillet

INSTRUCTIONS:
Heat butter in a skillet and sauté the mushrooms, red pepper and onion for a few minutes.
Insert the ingredients into a slow cooker.
Add the chilli powder and vegetable broth and cook on high for 30 minutes.
Toss in the rice into the slow cooker, mix well and cook for another 15 minutes,
Add the soy sauce, garlic and the lime juice in a bowl and place the salmon top side down in the sauce and leave for about 15 minutes.
Once properly seasoned, pour the liquid into the slow cooker.
Place the salmon on top and cook for another 1 hour until done.

Cooking for One Creole Chicken in the Slow Cooker

INGREDIENTS:
1 skinless, boneless chicken breast fillets
Salt and pepper to taste
Cajun seasoning to taste
3.5 oz tin chopped tomatoes
1/4 stalk celery, diced
1/4 green pepper, diced
1/2 cloves garlic, minced
1/4 onion, diced
1 oz mushrooms, sliced
1 fresh green chilli, seeded and chopped
INSTRUCTIONS:
Insert the chicken seasoned with salt, pepper and Cajun seasoning into a slow cooker.
Toss in the tomatoes, green pepper, celery, garlic, mushrooms, onion and green chilli.
Mix all the ingredients together and cook for 2-4 hours on low.

Cooking For One Slow Cooker Pulled Chicken

INGREDIENTS:
1/2 large skinless, boneless chicken breast fillets
3 tsp ketchup
1/4 Tbsps. mustard
1/4 tsps. lemon juice
1/8 tsp. garlic granules
3 tsp maple syrup
¼ Tbsps. Worcestershire sauce
1/8 tsp. chilli powder
1/8 tsp. cayenne pepper
1/8 dashes hot sauce or to taste
1 rolls or baps, split

INSTRUCTIONS:
Place the meat into the bottom of a slow cooker.

Add the mustard, ketchup, garlic granules, lemon juice, maple syrup, chilli powder, cayenne pepper, Worcestershire sauce and hot sauce into a bowl and combine well.

Pour the sauce over the meat, reduce the heat to low and allow to cook for 1 hour.

Once the meat is cooked, shred the meat using a fork and leave for another 15 minutes.

Serve the meat with sauce.

Cooking For One Chicken Jalfrezi Slow Cooker

INGREDIENTS:
1 chicken breast fillets, diced, or thighs
1/2 Tbsps. plain flour
1/4 large onion, roughly chopped
1/2 cloves garlic, roughly chopped
1/2 fresh green chillies, chopped
3.5 oz tin passata
1/4 tsp. ground coriander
1/4 tsp. ground cumin
1/4 or 2 red or green peppers, roughly chopped
1/8 tsp. chilli powder
1/2 whole fresh red chillies (optional)
1/2 tsps. garam masala
1/2 tsps. curry powder

INSTRUCTIONS:
Rub the chicken with flour and brown in a skillet.

Place all the ingredients in a slow cooker and cook for 1 hour on low.

Once the meat is no longer pink in the middle the meat is ready for use.

Add more corn-flour if the sauce is too thin until the required consistency is reached.

Cooking For One Slow Cooker Chicken And Mushroom Curry

INGREDIENTS:

2 chicken thigh pieces

1/2 chopped onion

1/2 tin condensed low fat mushroom soup

3 oz sliced mushrooms

1 tsps. curry powder (or to taste)

1 tsps. dried mixed herbs

INSTRUCTIONS:

Place the chicken in a skillet and brown well.

Insert the browned chicken into the slow cooker.

Toss in the onions and sauté until soft and tender.

Mix with the chicken.

Add the balance ingredients into the slow cooker.

Combine well and cook for over 3 hours.

Cooking For One Slow Cooker Easy Beef Curry

INGREDIENTS:
Vegetable oil
1 onions, diced
1/2 tsp. garam masala
1/2 tsp. ground cumin
1/2 tsp. ground coriander
1 ½ heaped Tbsps. Patak's® hot Madras curry paste
7 oz diced stew beef
Small squirt tomato puree
Salt and pepper

INSTRUCTIONS:
Pour the oil into a frying pan, heat and sauté the onions for about 5 minutes.
Toss in the spices and curry paste and combine well until fragrant.
Add the diced beef into the slow cooker.
Fold the onion mixture into the slow cooker.
Pour the tomato puree and water to cover the beef.
Mix all the ingredients together.
Cover with lid and cook for more than 24 hours.
Just prior to one hour of serving, take off the lid.
Increase the heat to high and allow the mixture to thicken.
Adjust seasonings.
Can be served with naan bread, rice, poppadums, chutneys etc.

Cooking For One Slow Cooker Fusion Pork Curry

INGREDIENTS:

9 oz diced pork

1/4 potatoes, peeled and cut into chunks

Oil for frying

1 medium onions, quartered

1/4 tsp. ground cumin

1/4 tsp. ground coriander

1/4 tsp. garam masala

1/4 knob butter

1/2 cardamom pods

.5 oz medium madras curry powder

salt and black pepper to taste

1/4 Tbsp. plain flour

2 Tbsps. frozen petit pois

good handful cauliflower florets

1 eggs, hard boiled and halved

INSTRUCTIONS:

Switch the slow cooker on to low.

Add the pork and the potatoes.

Pour a little oil into a skillet and sauté the onions until soft.

Stir in the coriander, cumin and garam masala and a bit more oil.

Combine until fragrant and transfer to the slow cooker.

Use the same skillet, melt the butter on a low heat.

Stir in the flour and the curry powder and combine well.

Add the water in degrees and prepare the sauce similar to a pouring cream.

Pour the liquid over the ingredients and mix well.

Cook for about 2 hours and during the last ¼ hour toss in the peas and cauliflower.

Can be served with hard boiled eggs.

Cooking For One Slow Cooker Beef Rogan Josh Masala

INGREDIENTS:
Oil for cooking
6 oz diced beef
1/2 large red onion, sliced
1 garlic cloves, diced
Salt and black pepper, to taste
1 Tbsps. rogan josh masala seasoning
1 potatoes, peeled and diced
1/2 cup lukewarm water
1 tins chopped tomatoes

INSTRUCTIONS:
Use a little oil and sauté the beef until brown.
Add the onion, garlic, salt, pepper and 1 tbsp of josh seasoning. Mix well.
Place the potatoes into the bottom of the slow cooker.
Insert the browned meat on top of the potatoes.
Stir the balance seasoning with water and add with tomatoes to the slow cooker.
Cook for 3 hours on medium until the beef is tender.

Cooking For One Slow Cooker Lamb And Sweet Potato Curry

INGREDIENTS:
2 oz lean lamb
1/4red onion, chopped
1/4 clove of garlic, chopped
1/8 tsp. turmeric
1/2 Tbsp. garam marsala spice mix
1/4 tsp. dried chilli flakes
2 tsp stock
1.7 oz chopped fresh tomatoes
1 sweet potato, peeled and diced

INSTRUCTIONS:
Place the lamb in a skillet and allow to brown on both sides.
Transfer the browned meat into a slow cooker.
Use the same skillet and fry the garlic, onion and spices prior to placing in the slow cooker.
Add the tomatoes, diced potato and pour the stock over the ingredients.
Cook on high for 1 hour.
Can be served with nan bread or rice.

Cooking for One Slow-Cooker Sweet-and-Sour Country Ribs

INGREDIENTS:
1/8 cup ketchup
1/8 cup packed light-brown sugar
1/8 cup cider vinegar
1/4 Tbsp. mustard powder
1/8 tsp. cayenne pepper
Coarse salt and ground pepper
1/2 pounds country-style pork ribs, separated into single ribs
Barbecue sauce, for serving (optional)
INSTRUCTIONS:
Whisk together sugar, ketchup, vinegar, mustard powder, cayenne, 1/8 tsp salt and 1/8 tsp pepper.
Insert the ribs into the slow cooker and mix with the sauce.
Lay the ribs, bone side facing upwards in a single layer.
Cover with lid and cook for 1 hour on high.
Serve the ribs with pan juices and if required can be served with barbecue sauce as well.

Cooking for One Slow-Cooker Chicken Tikka Masala

INGREDIENTS:

4-oz. can crushed tomatoes

1/4 medium onion, chopped

1/2 cloves garlic, chopped

1/2 Tbsps. tomato paste

1/2 tsps. garam masala (Indian spice blend)

kosher salt and black pepper

1/4 pounds boneless, skinless chicken thighs (about 8)

1/8 English cucumber, halved and thinly sliced

1/8 cup fresh cilantro leaves

1/4 Tbsp. fresh lemon juice

1/4 cup basmati or some other long-grain white rice

1/8 cup heavy cream

INSTRUCTIONS:

Place the tomatoes, onion, garlic, garam masala, tomato paste, ¾ tsp salt and ¼ tsp pepper in a bowl.

Lay the meat on top of the vegetables, cover and cook the meat until tender for 2 hours on low or 1 hour on high.

Toss the cilantro and cucumber in a small bowl with the lemon juice and ¼ tsp of salt and ¼ tsp pepper.

Cover and place in the refrigerator up to 2 hours.

Twenty minutes prior to serving, prepare the rice according to the instructions.

At the time of serving, add the cream into the meat.

Serve with rice and cucumber relish.

Conclusion

Thank you again for downloading this book!
I hope this book was able to help you discover some amazing Cooking For One Recipes. The next step is to get cooking!!!

45832323R00034

Made in the USA
San Bernardino, CA
18 February 2017